Life Lessons of African Proverbs

Festus E. Obiakor

Valdosta State University

Dike Okoro

Concordia University Wisconsin

Gathogo M. Mukuria

University of Nairobi, Kenya

Publisher's information, address:
Cissus World Press, P.O. Box 240865, Milwaukee, WI 53224
www.cissusworldpressbooks.com

ISBN: 978-0-997-8689-7-5
First published in the U.S.A by Cissus World Press LLC

CISSUS WORLD PRESS BOOKS.

Printed in the United States of America.

        Distributor:
    African Books Collective Ltd
    Email: orders@africanbookscollective.com
    Website: http://www.africanbookscollective.com

FOREWORD

As a former Dean and Department Chair at several institutions of higher learning, infatuated with the power and potential of words and the ways in which they give birth to old and new ideas, I am blown away by this unique book, *Life Lessons of African Proverbs.* It is an authentic and aspirational volume of formulaic prose designed to advance our meaning-making muscles.

An ephemeral look at the word "proverb" reveals a derivation of Latin origin: *proverbium* – a word that literally means "to put forth words (of salience and significance)." In this book, Obiakor, Mukuria, and Okoro are successful in supplying us with a treatise of ancestral words designed to make better sense of optimizing how we understand ourselves and others in a way that promotes harmony, honors diversity, and honestly perpetuates truth; the truth about humanity.

Life Lessons of African Proverbs is the best illustration of the balance between artistry, wisdom, intuition, and intellect as it relates to the complexity and beauty of the human experience. I offer these sentiments without equivocation because of the three decades of quality scholarship furnished by Obiakor. Fascinatingly, his colleagues, Mukuria and Okoro are also scholars who have continued to use their voices to push the envelope in their respective disciplines. Their body of works has challenged, agitated, and most of all elevated the hearts, minds, and spirits of students, colleagues, and critics all over the world. As a witness to the endemic and perpetual provocation of their thoughtful concepts and ideas over the course of their scholarly careers, I find this work to be a preeminent offering to the academic community, but useful for all communities that value the sagacity and insightful acumen of those who came before us. And, we are not talking about average individuals, but the mothers and fathers of civilization as we know it – surely, their ponderings and musings have value and significance for how we as individuals govern our steps to enhancement – otherwise *known as being, holistically, better than what we were.*

In a scholastic space that typically values deconstructive and parochial examination as anointed processes for authentic study and research, this book solidly reminds us that we, human-beings, are more alike than unalike; and that we share more in common than not in common. The dexterity and multidimensionality of this book's fluidity in application across disciplines cannot be overstated or trivialized. Obiakor, Mukuria, and Okoro are masterful in their assembly of these proverbs.

This book should be at the coffee table of every enthusiastic reader. I urge the readers to enjoy this flavor of work and go beyond simplistic imaginations to meaningful worldly imaginations. Students, scholars, educators, and all should toast to this creative endeavor by Obiakor, Mukuria, and Okoro and share their evenings and meetings with *Life Lessons of African Proverbs*. Maybe, I mean, maybe, this book will help to make our world a wiser and peaceful place to live.

Dr. Sean Warner,
Professor (and Former Dean), COE
Clark Atlanta University, Atlanta, Georgia

PREFACE

Proverbs have been around human society for ages, and in Africa, they remain an integral part of people's lives. The very fact that they are culturally continuous, handed down from generation to generation, and serve a useful purpose in daily speech in Africa, goes a long way in showing how useful they are as self-enriching resource. It is therefore expedient to know that because of Africa's varied ethnic groups, some of the proverbs spoken or written by people from the continent have the tendency of being misunderstood or classified as ambiguous. Not to worry! With this book, we hope to provide for the reading public, students and educators, a harvest of proverbs that will intrigue, educate, and enrich individuals.

While editing the proverbs in this book, we thought about a famous adage shared by Chinua Achebe, Nigeria and Africa's foremost novelist, who asserted that "proverbs are the palm oil with which words are eaten." This powerful saying simply reaffirms the importance of proverbs in Africa and why they are cherished. The proverbs in this book communicate meanings and experiences that touch on different aspects of life. And, they are introductions to new ways to view life and its innumerable questions.

In this book, we arranged the proverbs in a way that should make reading palatable and joyful for readers. The good thing about covered themes and espoused ideas is that they can be appreciated by anybody, irrespective of culture, language, and national. The primary goal of this book is to disseminate knowledge and share the rich culture of Africa. Thus, one does not have to be African to appreciate the creative language at play in this book. These proverbs are edible fruits waiting to be eaten and enjoyed for their freshness and vitality. Where translation has been difficult, we have made concise effort to present an English version of these proverbs in a way that should make communication of ideas both pleasing and rewarding to the reader.

The number of life lessons in these proverbs illustrate how authentic and vital the proverbs selected for inclusion are to the goal of this project. Books with a serious message are meant to serve as a life-changing source. This book does exactly that and even more. We encourage readers to use the wisdom embedded in these proverbs to transform their lives and the lives of their loved ones and friends. African folklore, narratives, idiomatic expressions, and culture are weaved into short sentences that are rich with wisdom. While we acknowledge that books of this nature have been published, this collection serves a unique purpose of its timing and wide range of ideas that are traceable to various life-changing experiences and situations across the world.

As authors, we have considered the veracity of our creative expressions and have explored a wide range of topics to make this book a remarkable treasure. We hope readers will find in these proverbs fulfilling ideas that empower, inspire, motivate, and educate. Their subject-matter and literary expressions highlight the possibility of engaging one's mind in short sayings that state a general truth or offer a piece of advice to furnish one's mind with wisdom that guides actions.

Our world has gotten smaller and smaller because of our technological advancements. E-mails, google, tweets, and face books are now things of today; and they excite our imaginations and lures into simplicity. But, despite our world's advancements, we have generational destructive problems, struggles, and wars. We hope that this book of proverbs provides the solace and placidity that could heal our wounds, calm our worries, temper our nerves, and cathartically direct us towards unity, collaboration, and consultation. Even with all of differences, we live in ONE world---this is why a collection of this nature is critical to our daily existence. To all our readers, ONE LOVE!

Believe it or not, books of this nature are hard to write, especially since they cross disciplinary boundaries and magnify interdisciplinary perspectives. We thank our family members and friends for their support during this venture. In addition, we thank Dr. Sean Warner of Clark Atlanta University for writing the Foreword of this book. Hopefully, scholars, scientists, and students of all stripes will find this book funny, serious, and calming at the same time. But, specifically, we hope that this book will be used as a required or supplementary text by professors and students in Honor Colleges, Interdisciplinary Studies, African American Studies, African Studies/Programs, Multicultural Studies, Foreign Language Departments, to mention a few. Again, ONE LOVE!

Festus E. Obiakor
Dike Okoro
Gathogo M. Mukuria

TABLE OF CONTENTS

Foreword by Sean Warner...........................p. i
Preface..p. iii
Proverb #1 and Life Lesson........................ p.12

Proverb #2 and Life Lesson....................... p.12

Proverb #3 and Life Lesson....................... p.13

Proverb #4 and Life Lesson.......................p. 13

Proverb #5 and Life Lesson.......................p. 14

Proverb #6 and Life Lesson.......................p. 14

Proverb #7 and Life Lesson.......................p. 15

Proverb #8 and Life Lesson.......................p. 15

Proverb #9 and Life Lesson.......................p. 16

Proverb #10 and Life Lesson.......................p. 16

Proverb #11 and Life Lesson.......................p. 17

Proverb #12 and Life Lesson.......................p. 17

Proverb #13 and Life Lesson.......................p. 18

Proverb #14 and Life Lesson.......................p. 18

Proverb #15 and Life Lesson.......................p. 19

Proverb #16 and Life Lesson.......................p. 19

Proverb #17 and Life Lesson.......................p. 20

Proverb #18 and Life Lesson...................p. 20

Proverb #19 and Life Lesson...................p. 21

Proverb #20 and Life Lesson...................p. 21

Proverb #21 and Life Lesson...................p.22

Proverb #22 and Life Lesson...................p.22

Proverb #23 and Life Lesson............... ...p.23

Proverb #24 and Life Lesson...................p.23

Proverb #25 and Life Lesson...................p.24

Proverb #26 and Life Lesson...................p.24

Proverb #27 and Life Lesson...................p.25

Proverb #28 and Life Lesson...................p.25

Proverb #29 and Life Lesson...................p.26

Proverb #30 and Life Lesson...................p.26

Proverb #31 and Life Lesson...................p.27

Proverb #32 and Life Lesson...................p.27

Proverb #33 and Life Lesson...................p.28

Proverb #34 and Life Lesson...................p.28

Proverb #35 and Life Lesson...................p.29

Proverb #36 and Life Lesson...................p.29

Proverb #37 and Life Lesson..................p.30

Proverb #38 and Life Lesson..................p.30

Proverb #39 and Life Lesson..................p. 31

Proverb #40 and Life Lesson..................p. 31

Proverb #41 and Life Lesson..................p.32

Proverb #42 and Life Lesson..................p.32

Proverb #43 and Life Lesson..................p.33

Proverb #44 and Life Lesson..................p.33

Proverb #45 and Life Lesson..................p.34

Proverb #46 and Life Lesson..................p.34

Proverb #47 and Life Lesson..................p.35

Proverb #48 and Life Lesson..................p.35

Proverb #49 and Life Lesson..................p.36

Proverb #50 and Life Lesson..................p.36

Proverb #51 and Life Lesson..................p.37

Proverb #52 and Life Lesson..................p.37

Proverb #53 and Life Lesson..................p.38

Proverb #54 and Life Lesson..................p.38

Proverb #55 and Life Lesson..................p.39

Proverb #56 and Life Lesson....................p.39

Proverb #57 and Life Lesson....................p.40

Proverb #58 and Life Lesson....................p.40

Proverb #59 and Life Lesson....................p. 41

Proverb #60 and Life Lesson....................p. 41

Proverb #61 and Life Lesson....................p.42

Proverb #62 and Life Lesson....................p.42

Provcrb #63 and Life Lesson....................p.43

Proverb #64 and Life Lesson....................p.43

Proverb #65 and Life Lesson....................p.44

Proverb #66 and Life Lesson....................p.44

Proverb #67 and Life Lesson....................p.45

Proverb #68 and Life Lesson....................p.45

Proverb #69 and Life Lesson....................p.46

Proverb #70 and Life Lesson....................p.46

Proverb #71 and Life Lesson....................p.47

Proverb #72 and Life Lesson....................p.47

Proverb #73 and Life Lesson....................p.48

Proverb #74 and Life Lesson....................p.48

PROVERB #1: There is no ocean that lacks waves.

Life Lesson

This proverb is particularly used to remind all people that problems are a part of life. Clearly, life's problems are inevitable; and they occur in different ways. Our ability to handle them can determine how far we go in life.

PROVERB #2: When the leading bull is lame, the rest of the herd cannot drink water.

Life Lesson

A person in leadership is expected to be decisive, principled, and knowledgeable about what he/she is doing. This proverb implies that when a leader is weak and lacks leadership qualities, the followers are bound to be unproductive and cannot attain anything worthwhile.

PROVERB #3: Leadership is not witchcraft that is inherited.

Life Lesson

Leadership should not be perceived as an attribute that is genetically embedded in a particular family. If an individual has leadership qualities, it does not necessarily mean that his/her son or daughter will have similar qualities.

PROVERB #4: A person who fails to listen to his/her elders leads himself/herself to ruin.

Life Lesson

Wisdom is supposed to increase with age in many cultures since people acquire wisdom from their past experiences. While each generation thinks that it is better than the previous generation, it is imperative to assist young people to listen and carefully consider the advice they are given.

PROVERB #5: Two bulls do not live in the same shed.

Life Lesson

This proverb is used to describe how difficult it is for two competitors with similar abilities to come to terms. People must understand the interests of other community members with whom they interact in various situations. This understanding can greatly help them to bring everyone together to solve problems.

PROVERB #6: When one keeps you in the sun, you should put him/her in the shade.

Life Lesson

This proverb sets a high standard of living for community members. If someone mistreats you and you treat him/ her fairly, he/she is likely to change and be a friend. Hatred breeds hatred, but love conquers all!

PROVERB #7: An individual who does not learn from his/her parents will be taught by the world.

Life Lesson

This proverb is used to teach young people and children alike to listen to their parent(s). While parents are warm, tender, and loving in bringing up children, the world can be cruel, hard, and unforgiving.

PROVERB #8: One who does not travel assumes that only his/her mother cooks the most delicious dinner.

Life Lesson

This proverb encourages individuals to have broad perspectives about life. When people are close-minded, they cannot accept new ideas or accommodate diverse views about situations.

PROVERB #9: What leads to a person's downfall is really his/her close associates.

Life Lesson

This proverb cautions people to be careful in the way they select friends. Only people who are close to us can disappoint us. In addition, we must be careful about who we bring around to our family.

PROVERB #10: A person who is spied on by his/her closest neighbor cannot escape being caught.

Life Lesson

This proverb confirms that neighbors are expected to know each other well due to their close proximity to build each other. In the end, we must improve collaboration, consultation, and cooperation in our world. People can learn from each other through mentoring, role modeling, and positive imitation while still respecting individual differences.

PROVERB #11: A child who is yet to take control of the sword should not seek reasons for his/her father's death.

Life Lesson

This proverb reminds a child to be careful when challenging his/her elder in public. Maturity on how to deal with certain challenges in life is needed to handle misunderstandings with the elderly, in this case a child's father.

PROVERB #12: Doom is an ally to the mischievous.

Life Lesson

This proverb forewarns evil doers and mischievous people of the price of their actions. In the spiritual world, there is always a day of reckoning for every individual who derives pleasure in being mischievous.

PROVERB #13: When choosing friends, we must learn to trust our eyes and ears.

Life Lesson

This proverb simply reminds people to be wise when making friends, and to be attentive to details in order to identify true friends. It is not only by word of mouth that we know our true friends. We also have to trust our ears and believe in what we see.

PROVERB #14: If you think you have knowledge of all the troubles you have experienced in life, try to count the hair strands on your head.

Life Lesson

This proverb simply reminds human-beings that there are limitations to what one can retain in memory. It is an impossible task for one to assume that he/she can keep track of every obstacle experienced in life.

PROVERB #15: There is nothing to be ashamed of if one hunts vigorously and in the end has no catch.

Life Lesson

Oftentimes in life one might be pushed to the point of exhausting one's energy in order to achieve one's potential or goal. This is absolutely fine, as long as the end is justified.

PROVERB #16: Rivers are enlarged by their tributaries.

Life Lesson

This proverb means people become great because of the mandate they get from their followers. As a consequence, people must be cognizant that without collaboration of others, they will not be successful.

PROVERB #17: Look out before you act.

Life Lesson

This proverb forces us to examine all the consequences of our actions ahead of time. People should emphasize the need to carefully think and determine what the final consequences of their action will be before acting. This is because every action has a reaction and a consequence.

PROVERB #18: People who live at the base of a tree know what nourishes it.

Life Lesson

There is nothing better than learning through experience. When one lives through hardships and problems, he/she is forced to be creative. This proverb informs us to know how best to tackle a problem. In other words, we cannot solve problems unless we know what they are.

PROVERB #19: Never underestimate your enemy or opponent.

Life Lesson

This proverb indicates that it is easy to underestimate other people's potential. For example, if a basketball team is playing against an opponent, it should practice vigorously to win the game.

PROVERB #20: It is the one who has tasted the drink that knows its flavor.

Life Lesson

This proverb shows that there is a difference between theory and practice. True learning takes place through practical experience. People must emphasize the need to integrate theory and practice as much as possible. We must live up to our words through actions.

PROVERB #21: One does not need to spell out everything to an intelligent person.

Life Lesson

This proverb explains that knowledge is the power that illuminates in the darkness. An intelligent person can interpret and grasp the meaning of words quickly. The ability to derive meaning from the written and spoken words should not be taken for granted.

PROVERB #22: Doing things in a hurry can be counterproductive.

Life Lesson

This proverb is used as a cautionary measure to individuals who always do things in a hurry. It also indicates that when tasks are performed with caution, the final product is usually good. Additionally, when something is done hurriedly, some details are sometimes left out, making the final product to be bad or inaccurate.

PROVERB #23: Sliding is not falling.

Life Lesson

In real life, there are many ups and downs. At times, people meet barriers on their paths and they slide. When one slides, it does not mean that he/she has fallen; and as a result, he/she cannot give up. This proverb gives hope and second chance to a person going through challenges and problems in life.

PROVERB #24: Birds look for one another when landing but scatter when flying.

Life Lesson

This proverb indicates that unity is only maintained when people act as a group. For example, during riot people may engage in destructive group behavior, but when law enforcement comes to the scene, people flee individually. In addition, this pro verb also means that one's individually deserves to be protected.

PROVERB #25: People who are not united are beaten by one club.

Life Lesson

The proverb illustrates the importance of unity. Unity is strength and if people go to war without it, they will be defeated. Unless leaders enhance that common purpose by uniting, goals and objectives cannot be achieved.

PROVERB #26: What is mine is better than what is yours.

Life Lesson

This proverb teaches us to be self-reliant and believe in ourselves. The purpose of life is to enlighten the mind and equip ourselves with confidence and skills that would enable us to be self-reliant and productive citizens.

PROVERB #27: Too much haste breaks the yam's tuber.

Life Lesson

Many a time, people have the tendency to perform tasks hurriedly. When things are done in a hurry, minor details are sometimes left out, making the final outcome to be unfavorable.

PROVERB #28: One who desires all misses all.

Life Lesson

Selective attention helps an individual to focus on the most salient matters. In life, one has to be careful in selecting precisely the stimulus of interest. There is a big difference between want and need; and failure to understand these results in total confusion.

PROVERB #29: A procrastinator never gets anything accomplished on time

Life Lesson

There are people who have great ideas but lack the wherewithal to implement them. In life, we must realize the danger of procrastination and try to embark on tasks on time. Tasks do not do themselves; people do them.

PROVERB #30: A person who builds hope on his/her family's wealth dies as a poor person.

Life Lesson

This proverb encourages individuals to emphasize the need for working hard to achieve their goals. In life, we do not want to live on false hopes. Family reputation is important; however, individual reputation is also critical.

PROVERB #31: Where there is a will, there is a way.

Life Lesson

It is important for people to understand the resiliency of the human spirit. In life, there are times when individuals find themselves surrounded by impossibilities. This proverb is a reminder that if one has a will, there are ways to solve problems. Individual abilities plus personal can enable an average person to excel.

PROVERB #32: Where there is smoke, there is fire.

Life Lesson

Smoke always originates where there is fire. In life, whenever there are rumors, there might be some elements of reality. It is good for us to carefully know how those rumors originated. Perhaps, problems can be solved when they are tackled on time.

PROVERB #33: The frogs' eyes do not deter cattle from drinking water.

Life Lesson

This proverb is an encouragement that one should not stop doing something worthwhile because of criticisms. In life, people do not criticize someone who is idle; they criticize those doing something. Finally, we must not allow ourselves to be deterred by criticisms, especially if we are working hard to do the right thing.

PROVERB #34: A good item sells itself.

Life Lesson

In life, goodness attracts attention like a magnet. It goes without saying that good behavior or character is easily noted in the community. In addition, we must emphasize and teach the importance of good behavior in our communities.

PROVERB #35: The voice of the community is the voice of God.

Life Lesson

There is reciprocal connection between the community and God. The community therefore endeavors to do what is good and pleasing to God. In other words, the will of the community is considered to be congruent with the will of God. In life, we must reach out to all community members. Together we stand and divided we fall.

PROVERB #36: Wisdom is greater than strength.

Life Lesson

Wisdom and strength are two different things. Physical strength does not necessarily mean that an individual can make sound judgment. Wisdom plays a critical role in the way we deal with our fellow humans and make judgments about them.

PROVERB #37: A self-made fool is worse than a natural one.

Life Lesson

When one acts or plays a role that is not his/hers, things are bound to go wrong. To be deliberately dim-witted is worse than being a natural fool. In life, we must be prudent in dealing with issues and situations.

PROVERB #38: You reap what you sow.

Life Lesson

This proverb has a biblical allusion. With determination and personal tenacity, individuals achieve their set goals. On the contrary, those who do not work hard may not achieve so much. In life, we must strive to help others set high but realistic goals. In addition, we must stress that our success and failures are based on our efforts and abilities to change.

PROVERB #39: If you do not fill up a crack, you will have to build a wall.

Life Lesson

When there is a crack on the wall, it should be filled before the entire wall falls. In life, we must be vigilant in solving our problems before they get out of hand. Put another way, we must be abreast of the times to advance our community, society, and world.

PROVERB #40: A mud hut cannot withstand an earthquake.

Life Lesson

For us to do well, we need to be well-grounded to weather the storms of life. Nothing is easy in life if it is worth learning. In other words, the more prepared we are, the better for us.

PROVERB #41: A caring husband sleeps peacefully at home.

Life Lesson

A husband who treats his wife with respect and care will find his stay at home a peaceful and joyful experience. This proverb teaches that which is known in life: do to others as you would have them do to you.

PROVERB #42: The wise parent teaches his child good manners by talking less.

Life Lesson

In life, children pick up habits and mannerisms through observation. Hence a parent must act in ways that will pass on good mannerisms to his/her child. As the saying goes, children grow up thinking and acting the way they were taught.

PROVERB #43: A good reputation gains attention like polish on shining shoes.

Life Lesson

An accomplished individual has no reason to hide his/her achievements. People will always take note of his/her individual efforts and contributions. As a result, we must keep our powders dry and try our best to be good roles on our communities.

PROVERB #44: Giving advice to a foolish person is like attempting to fetch water with a basket.

Life Lesson

There is no use spending time to advise a foolish person since experience teaches us that the foolish person always thinks he/she knows it all. To succeed in life, we must continue to learn. We literarily stop learning when we are dead.

PROVERB #45: A broken string of beads cannot regain the same length again.

Life Lesson

In this proverb, making of beads is likened to building a relationship. For example, friendship once broken is never the same, even after reconciliation. As humans, we must understand the importance of maintaining good relationship by enhancing harmony and true friendship.

PROVERB #46: A traveler always carries more than one bag.

Life Lesson

Based on this proverb, a traveler encounters many new situations that make traveling susceptible to dangers. The uncertainty of what to encounter in his/her trip dictates adequate preparation. As humans, we are all travelers who must be willing to learn new ideas and broaden our perspectives.

PROVERB #47: Water follows in the path of least resistance.

Life Lesson

In life, many people prefer to get things done as quickly as possible without following the correct procedure. For example, to get a good job, one has to go through rigors of educational processes. Simply, there are no short cuts in life; and for one to succeed, one has to work with vigor and consistency.

PROVERB #48: Firewood that is in the store laughs at the firewood burning in the fireplace.

Life Lesson

It is easy for people to laugh at someone in certain situations not envisioning that they can be in similar situations. According to this proverb, we are challenged as human-beings to be humble and be nonjudgmental towards others because no one is immune from unfortunate situations.

PROVERB #49: Do not engage in war without weapon.

Life Lesson

It is always important to count the cost before one engages in any project. In sports, each team usually prepares well with the hope that it will outplay its opponent. In life, we must prepare because poor planning prevents poor performance.

PROVERB #50: A dancer who is unable to perform blames the stony courtyard.

Life Lesson

It is imperative for someone to be honest and principled in word and deed. Unfortunately, some individuals look for excuses and engage in the blame game to evade their duty. Being honest and taking responsibility in what we do is what makes us admirable.

PROVERB #51: The early bird catches the worm.

Life Lesson

People have different ways of performing tasks. More often than not, those who plan to do their work early do it with great dedication and determination and the final product is normally impressive. Logically, an early traveler arrives at his/her destination early.

PROVERB #52: Many eyes see better than one eye.

Life Lesson

Collaboration and consultation are good decision-making tools. When a number of people look at the same thing from different perspectives, they are more likely to come up with different views. As a consequence, they feel good that they are given the simple opportunity to share their own view. In life, this leads to partnership and unity of purpose.

PROVERBS #53: A person who fetches water from a river should not insult crocodiles.

Life Lesson

Human-beings seem to be forgetful of their struggles, especially when they think that they have arrived. Such an attitude may be detrimental to their personal relationships with others. In life, we must realize that we are all growing. This means that we must treat people with respect and dignity.

PROVERB #54: A person who is afraid to ask questions does not learn.

Life Lesson

There are people who, due to their own pride, assume that they know everything. In life, there is always something to learn. We must encourage people to seek the truth or new knowledge. To make it in life, we must continue to learn.

PROVERB #55: Fire is not extinguished with fire.

Life Lesson

We realize that certain actions lead to certain reactions. There is no point in escalating a situation that is already bad. In life, disagreements are not unusual among people; however, we must be ready to compromise as needed.

PROVERB #56: No one can make an appointment with death.

Life Lesson

The concept of death is rarely discussed even though it is inevitable. This means that we must try to live our lives better so that posterity will acknowledge our contributions.

PROVERB #57: A bee does not start with the honeycomb.

Life Lesson

Looking at a bee in a honeycomb one wonders how such a small creature is able to make honey. Lots of collaborative efforts and teamwork are involved in the process. We need to learn the importance of patience and be content to start with small steps to solve problems.

PROVERB #58: Success comes with repeated efforts.

Life Lesson

Many people assume that success is something that is easily achieved. On the contrary, success comes with hard work and patience. Many successful people have failed a number of times before they gradually started to succeed. In life, we must understand that patience is a virtue.

PROVERB #59: Taking an empty net home does not make one a bad fisherman.

Life Lesson

In life, people have their off days when things do not go as planned. Having the ability to understand this situation helps us to mold our characters in life. In other words, we must never allow ourselves to get frustrated, especially when things do not work out.

PROVERB #60: In a time of war, wisdom is treasured more than diamonds.

Life Lesson

Critical thinking is important in life. We must be prudent in all our actions. When faced with difficulties in life, we are more likely to treasure good advice. When we stop learning, we stop thinking.

PROVERB #61: It takes a whole village to raise a child.

Life Lesson

The community must work together to solve community problems. Educators and leaders are part of a team, and they must work together in partnership to create ideas and advance the community. Interactions are made functional and operational when everyone is a part of the team.

PROVERB #62: When you wrestle someone to the ground, you also wrestle yourself to the ground because when you stand up, he will stand up with you.

Life Lesson

Problems are solved when people work together. Progressive and regressive decisions affect everyone; and how, when, and why we are involved must be clearly delineated. Educators and leaders must understand that the decisions they make have far-reaching effects on everyone. "Each One, Reach One" should be the motto of any educator and leader.

PROVERB #63: A tree cannot make a forest.

Life Lesson

A person is a part of a community and his or her interests are tied to community interests. Excellent educators and leaders must collaborate, consult, and cooperate for a system to be functional. Without teamwork and partnership, no organization can solve problems, advance its mission and vision, and maintain stability.

PROVERB #64: When mother cow is chewing grass, the younger ones look at her mouth.

Life Lesson

Observation is a critical learning-teaching technique. It is no surprise that observation is an important aspect of education and leadership. We must be prepared to learn from others. In other words, educators and leaders are role models who can influence how their students, colleagues, and team members behave. We teach and lead by modeling appropriate behavior.

PROVERB #65: Truth is life.

Life Lesson

In life, people value and respect the truth when matters of opposing opinions are tabled for discussion and resolution. Likewise, people who embrace the truth have little or no reason to be labeled as negative role models in their community.

PROVERB #66: Life is in the ears.

Life Lesson

Active listening is one of the basic ingredients of human communications and interactions. When we listen, we build communities. Great educators and leaders listen to students, parents, colleagues, supervisors, communities, and governments. In addition, they design programs that enhance collaboration, consultation, and cooperation.

PROVERB #67: To come and eat is not to come and work!

Life Lesson

It is important to know that there is time for everything, a time to celebrate and a time to work! The invitation to eat must be honored by community members. As educators, we must know the difference; there is a time to play and a time to work. Leaders must know when to reward their team members, and educators must know when to reward their students.

PROVERB #68: A person who does not concede defeat is not a good sport.

Life Lesson

Failure can have rewarding after-effects in life. It can be rehabilitating to suffer from defeat—we learn a lot from failure and defeat. When there is failure in our lives, we learn from it and make sure it rarely occurs. Clearly, it is not how many times we are defeated, it is what we have learned after we are defeated.

PROVERB #69: A person who praises the rain has been rained on.

Life Lesson

It is common knowledge that experience is powerful. Without experiential knowledge, there is no foundation to work with. It is self-responsible to develop knowledge. You cannot talk about anything truthfully until you have experienced and experimented on it!

PROVERB #70: It is not the load that breaks us down; it is the way we carry it.

Life Lesson

How we do what we do is absolutely important. It is our responsibility to understand and value the inevitability of crisis and stressors in whatever we do; however, how we manage them can create positive pathways for success.

PROVERB #71: A good name shines in the dark.

Life Lesson

Goodness is next to Godliness. Integrity mattes; and it important that we understand our role in maintaining our good name. In addition, we must maintain good and uncontaminated honesty in our interactions with people different from us.

PROVERB #72: Where you live is where you protect.

Life Lesson

Self-protection is a part of self-responsibility. It involves the ability to respect one's boundaries and deal with one's problems. Since self-protection is a life necessity, it behooves us to make our environments conducive for all. In our efforts to protect our domains, we must make them conducive to others. Self-protection is important, especially when it is devoid of exclusivity.

PROVERB #73: Money is the beauty of a man.
Life Lesson

Typically, men are viewed as handsome and women are viewed as beautiful; and life cannot be sustained without money. Clearly, it is the responsibility of people to provide money to bring to fruition all human activities and life-sustaining programs. In the end, we must view it as our human responsibility to provide and manage money for programmatic excellence.

PROVERB #74: You can cry all you want, but you cannot cry out blood.

Life Lesson

There is always a limit to what we can do. As a result, we must be responsible for our own actions and when to take our losses and move on. It is self-responsible to know what to do and what the consequences of our actions will be.

About the Authors:

Festus Obiakor (PhD) is a professor at
Valdosta State University. He is the author of three volumes of poetry and several inspirational books, including the book, *100 Multicultural Proverbs* and *It Even Happens in Good Schools* (Crown Books).

Dike Okoro (PhD) is a professor of English at
Concordia University and the author of three volumes of poetry and the editor of several anthologies of short stories and poetry, including *Speaking for the Generation: Contemporary Short Stories from Africa* (Trenton: Africa World Press, 2010).

Gathogo Mukuria (PhD) is a professor at the
University of Nairobi, Kenya. He has a keen interest in multicultural education and has published articles focusing on making a difference in the lives of children and youth in urban schools.

Printed in the United States
By Bookmasters